HENRY
THE HELPER

JESSICA PAULSEN

To my life's adventure, Bobby
And, of course, to Henry.

AuthorHouse™
1663 Liberty Drive
Bloomington, IN 47403
www.authorhouse.com
Phone: 1 (800) 839-8640

Because of the dynamic nature of the Internet, any web addresses or links contained in this book may have changed since publication and may no longer be valid. The views expressed in this work are solely those of the author and do not necessarily reflect the views of the publisher, and the publisher hereby disclaims any responsibility for them.

This book is printed on acid-free paper.

ISBN: 978-1-7283-3486-8 (sc)
ISBN: 978-1-7283-3487-5 (e)

Print information available on the last page.

Published by AuthorHouse 11/07/2019

authorHOUSE®

Henry The Helper

Some puppies grow up to be small. Some puppies grow up to be big.

Some puppies grow up to be fluffy or Curly.
And some puppies grow up to be heroes.

This puppy is named Henry.

He is just a baby now,
but someday he is going
to have a big job.

3

This is Jessica. She may not look it, but she is very sick. So she is looking for a dog that can help her to do all the things she can't.

Henry and his brothers and sisters are all very different. Some of them are shy. Some of them are playful. Some of them are sleepy.

5

But then there is Henry. He is curious, gentle, and smart. He is the perfect match for Jessica.

6

Henry was ready for his new home. He packed up his toys and his blanket, said goodbye to his brothers and sisters, and was on his way.

Training Week I
Sit   Down
Walking Nicely

There was so much to learn about being a helper dog!

Together with Jessica, he began his lessons.

8

They started with the easy part. Being a good dog meant getting lots of treats! "This is great!" Henry thought.

Soon he would get treats for sitting, lying down, and walking nicely by Jessica's side.

Getting a treat wasn't always so easy. Henry had to remember a lot and would get confused.

Sometimes during lessons, he wanted to keep playing instead.

He enjoyed exploring the house, meeting other dogs, and playing tug with his leash.

But Henry always knew when it was time to get back to work. Not before long, Henry was able to retrieve items for Jessica. He learned how to behave around his dog friends. He also realized that leashes were not meant for playing.

Jessica was very proud.

Every day Henry would help Jessica
with chores around the house.

He would remind her when it was time to take her medicine. He was always right by her side in case she needed something.

One day Jessica was feeling very sick. She told Henry to, "Go get help!"

18

Henry knew just
what to do. He ran
across the house and
returned with help.

"Good job, buddy," said Jessica's husband.

20

Just after Henry's second birthday, a special day arrived.

He was ready to be measured for his first helper dog harness.

Henry could hardly contain his excitement when he wore his harness for the first time.

All of his lessons had been worth it!

Henry was ready to show the world what a good helper he was. He gathered his harness and brought Jessica her shoes. When she asked, "Are you ready to go?", with a wag of his tail, they were off.

Henry knew he would be
the best helper dog the
world had ever seen.

About the Author

Jessica Paulsen is just like any other 20-something-year-old that is if the other 20-something-year-olds spend every day with chronic illness and a Golden Retriever. After spending nearly a year in bed, she decided she was going to make the best of her situation. Jessica began sharing her story across social media in 2017, finding her way into Peoples Magazine and Good Morning America. She became a mouthpiece for service dog handlers and those suffering from both mental and physical illnesses. As she continues to pursue her dreams of travel and adventure, she is giving a firsthand look into what it means to be differently-abled.

Printed in the United States
By Bookmasters